The Gloucestershire Pomona Series

MEMORIES OF LIFE AS AN ITINERANT

by
Martin Hayes

To Libby - who was there

FOREWORD

by Jim Chapman
series editor

The earlier volumes in the Gloucestershire *Pomona* series focussed upon the fruit varieties found in the orchard. Volume 5 will focus upon the orchard itself and on the harvesting, transport, packaging and sale of the products of the orchard.

It is intended to publish the individual sections as they are written, before eventually binding these together as volume 5 of the Gloucestershire *Pomona*.

The first part is a very idiosyncratic account of a group of stalwarts of the industry, the itinerant labourer, by Martin, drawing on his personal experiences as an itinerant. Martin's account introduces us to life on the road and work in the field. In the final section he explains why this way of life is drawing to an end and the reasons he personally became a householder.

Agriculture and particularly the orchard industry has for centuries depended upon the labour of skilled workers, who travelled the country to carry out the seasonal tasks of the farm. John Moore in *Portrait of Elmbury* pays tribute to the casual labourer – the odd-jobber who could turn his hand to anything. The modern-day notion that this independent community is a threat, that should be harried and encouraged to move on, is a sad reflection of present times. They fulfilled an essential need in our orchards and fields, a need that is now increasingly met by migrants from eastern Europe.

Thankfully the skills Martin learnt from a lifetime working in orchards, are not lost. He now devotes his time to running the training days in orchards cared for by the Gloucestershire Orchard Trust.

Life on the road
Grabs hold,
Of your very being.
To most it's a way of Life,
Whilst some are only fleeing.

Martin Hayes Poems and other stuff

CHAPTER 1

EARLY START

I was twelve when I first walked on to a potato field. Little did I know what the future would hold! You would be mistaken in thinking I came from a tough travelling family. The reality is the polar opposite. My father was a sergeant in the army and my mother a seamstress. We were living in a large detached house in Catterick, Richmondshire. My introduction to the joys of picking potatoes, tongue firmly in cheek, was due to my failure as a newspaper boy. I got a paper-round but lasted only one day, having got hopelessly lost. This in itself was ironic as later I would briefly run a Readers Digest delivery service!

It was summer 1968 and to this point I had been to thirteen different schools in England, Malaya, Singapore and Hong Kong. As a school boy, life couldn't be more exciting. In an attempt to keep us concentrating on studies, my parents tried to contain this excitement by not telling us when we were moving. Any new posting for my Dad would be relayed to us by the headmaster on the day we were leaving school! The outcome of this constant moving was, for me, not good with regard to academia.

My siblings, on the other hand, have gone from strength to strength. My eldest brother works in Qatar teaching health and safety. My sister works with very poorly children. My younger brother is a psychiatric nurse. This is not to say I am in any way disappointed in my chosen path; on the contrary it suited me perfectly and at the ripe age of fifty-eight, I do talks on Itinerants with enthusiasm and a certain pride.

At the end of that summer of potato-picking, I perhaps did a week. My eldest brother, sister and I went to boarding school to help salvage some of our education. I believe that this was the turning point in my learning. Although my textbooks were almost empty, the school had a smallholding, which turned out to be my calling. I did very well at Rural Studies and got my highest mark at CSE in the exam. The Rural Studies teacher wanted me to go to a local college and board at the school but due to circumstances at home this was not possible.

My dad had left the army, whilst we were at boarding school, and had opened a shop in Bramcote, Nottingham. He was desperate for me to go and work for him which I did, being the first person in my year to leave the school. I remember sitting in the Housemaster's flat, drinking my first ever beer, at not even sixteen, to say farewell.

I had my first real experience of harvest work picking strawberries, whilst on a fortnight's holiday from the shop, in Sea Palling on the North Norfolk coast. I went with my elder brother, who had been the previous year, and some friends. When I think of these people, some of whom I still know, none carried on longer than their university years and all have careers far removed from mine. I went to Sea Palling for many years and have some great memories.

The shop never did well and on my eighteenth birthday my dad gave me a pair of work-boots and a donkey jacket and told me the shop was bankrupt. I moved in to my brother's shared house in Nottingham and signed on. I did various bits of work over that winter and set out in spring 1974 as an Itinerant. In those early years I kept my room in Nottingham and went home in winter.

CHAPTER 2

INSIDE OUT

Campfire scene

To most people it would be inconceivable to live all year round in a caravan. I would too, except that the outdoors was the biggest part of an itinerant's life. The camp-fire, when the weather permitted, formed an essential part of the living area and was where most travellers did their hosting. I remember well after the evening meal, deciding whether to 'keep the home fire burning' or go to another. There was an endless merry-go-round of people flitting from fire to fire, but the etiquette was always the same; bring a drink or something to smoke, a good story and never outstay your welcome.

We were not in a group and very often travelled to the next farm alone only to meet up with old friends whom we hadn't seen since the year before. As joyous as this was, there would always be the sad farewell at the end of the crop. These constant meetings and separations would also play a major part of life on the road and made the camp-fire an important place to talk of the year gone. Your caravan or lorry was another important place and showing people around your new set-up was a proud moment, albeit a brief one.

Life on the road was not always a barrel of laughs and at times it was hard, especially during the winter months. Although your living quarters always had a roaring fire, the outdoors would test your metal and that is why life on the road attracted some tough people. There were no toilets inside; cooking and defecating so close together is abhorrent to travellers, so the toilet is the first thing you removed when buying a caravan previously used for holidaying. It is true that some travellers do their business behind a hedge but the people I knew always carried a spade. Sorry to put it so bluntly, but I know you were curious! More on that subject later.

These homes would not have running water and this was a priority above everything. When arriving at the farm, all the water butts would be filled and the kettle would go on the gas hob, always run on propane (red bottles, as this is less likely to freeze). Then levelling the caravan and, if needed, digging the cesspit. The wood burner was the most important interior feature of any home and no expense was spared in getting the right one. Many a night in winter, folk would be sitting around discussing the merits of your burner with friends. Some people even made their own!

Cleanliness is always a slur on travellers by house dwellers. All I would say at the moment is yes, it was hard and sometimes you would go a number of days without a strip wash. Some farms had showers, but like most people one would always try especially if one were to go out.

Of course another major influence on an itinerant's life was the farmer 'Mein Host'. These came in all shapes and sizes. Some were purely business, some became good friends, while others ran off with your wife! But that's a different story, suffice to say that travellers are people with the same problems and misfortunes, only often they are there for all to see.

CHAPTER 3

THE FOREMAN'S HAT

The Foreman's hat a replica!

It wasn't until the later stages of my life as an itinerant that mobile phones were available, but by that time I had pretty much a full calendar. There were several ways to find work without a phone:

By introduction

This was a preferred method, as usually a friend had already found the work and would recommend the farmer to you and vice versa. There were not many jobs available and they would come about by other people leaving or an upturn in the farm production. One such farm was Cotswold Orchards near Evesham. There was a waiting-list of sorts to get a job here! When my girlfriend and I got invited, it was the start of the most steady and profitable period of work through the year and I credit this farm with the work I do to this day.

The library

Most of the jobs were found by trawling through phone directories in the local library before moving to any new area. This could be a costly affair as many of the farmers had sold up, especially in the early- to mid-eighties, to city types, had retired or become mechanised. Of course, with this method you were blindly going into a job, and few lasted longer than one season. Whoever got a job within the group at the time would get The Foreman's Hat, a tatty trilby with absolutely no power at all! I was usually the one who was motivated enough to get the work so it became mine.

One memorable job was hop-tying in Leigh, Worcestershire. Three of us left our "homes" during a lull in work and went off and lived in an old cattle wagon from the railway. The farmer was a very amusing chap, a Mr. Jay, who loved the fact he had three itinerants living in the yard and introduced us to all his farmer friends, a source of more work. After a number of days, he gave us straw to put down on the cold floor and even went as far as to put a slops bucket in a lean-to for us to use! Needless to say, the pub in the next village was our preferred method of waste disposal. Despite being away from home comforts we had a great time becoming so friendly with our host that he invited us to his wife's birthday bash, albeit in the shed at the back where the cider was kept, with food sent out. As party guests coming in and out, we thought we had fallen on our feet. The job lasted one season as the farmer sold up and now the Oast House, like so many, is now a dwelling.

By word of mouth

This was by far the most rewarding way and many of my jobs came through this. The Foreman's Hat still applied! There are generally areas best suited to growing certain crops, like early daffodils in Cornwall, plums in Evesham, apples in Kent, raspberries in Scotland. These would be talked about by other itinerants around fires. We would listen with interest and take down as much detail as possible and try to research it more. Always keen to add new areas to our itinerary, potato picking in St Davids, Pembrokeshire came about by this method. Of all the places I have lived and worked, it is here that had the biggest impact on me and I would consider home.

Arriving in a new area to cold-call farms was always going to be a risky process and this proved a tough one. Relying on lay-bys and wide verges to park up for the night, I realised how vulnerable life as a traveller really was and the importance of going to the same farm year after year became clear. I talk about this at the end of this recollection so won't go too far into it now.

On arrival at St Davids, we headed for the suggested pub, aptly named Farmers Arms, and started our enquiries. No one here thought it unusual for strangers to walk in asking about farmers looking to employ itinerants; it was the alternative job centre! After a number of drinks and a page full of contacts, we went back to our vehicles where our womenfolk were none too pleased by the length of time it had taken, but understood the negotiations involved. Over the next few days, armed with directions and names, we set about looking for work as potato pickers. It took quite a number of days too.

One of the perks of life on the road in those days was if you hated the job you didn't go back the next year. Although we relied on farmers for the work, the farmer relied on us as a source of cheap labour and there were lots of farms to choose from.

CHAPTER 4
───────────────────────────────

STRAWBERRY PICKING IN SEA PALLING NORFOLK

Strawberry pickers campsite (abandoned)

One of the delights of life as an itinerant was our summer work which inevitably found us by some seaside resort or holiday destination and Sea Palling was high up there. On the North Norfolk coast there were lots of strawberry farms servicing a large jam processing plant at Tunstall. It was in this area where I got hooked into life as an itinerant. When I first went to Sea Palling, the main strawberry grower and owner of the jamming plant was a Mr. Plaice who supplied a campsite with toilets, shower and a TV/games barn. I realised in later years what a luxury this was. As we were on the campsite we were obliged to pick for the farmer but this was very loosely monitored and open to abuse.

The day started with a fire to make tea and toast, usually made with a campfire Breville toaster gadget clamped together and placed directly into the embers. Then a bike ride to the field of work; anything up to ten miles away. On arrival you were allocated your row and given punnets to hold 6lbs, then you would start. You could carry four punnets at a time and you cashed them in for tokens worth 17.5p, 20p, 22.5p and 25p, depending on the crop and what was decided on the day. At the end of the shift, you could cash your tokens in or keep them as a form of saving; each one colour coded for the price that day. There were of course ways to out-wit the gangers with seedpods, stones etc with the inevitable consequences if caught. The gangers were hard-nosed Gypsy types who, at the time, scared the pants off us! The punnets were emptied into a trailer to be taken to the factory when full. Foreign students manned the factory and were crammed into caravans. They were paid little but charged a lot for accommodation. Some things never change!

Picking strawberries was a back-breaking job and not at all like the strawberry picking nowadays. Crawling on your hands and knees up rows only to reach the end and turn around. It was soul destroying but a means to an end. Picking rarely went on beyond 2pm so there was plenty of time to enjoy the tearooms of the Norfolk Broads or the beach. Some days when we were feeling lazy we would pick to the end of our row, cash in, go back to the row as if we hadn't finished, fall to our knees crawl to the end, roll in to the ditch or undergrowth and belly crawl to the road.

Twice a week there was a disco at the factory where we were taken by bus to meet the foreigners. This proved a mistake by the bosses as people talk and they realised the exploitation and it lead to a massive strike in which gunshots were fired and a friend's leg being broken by a tractor running over him. The strike made the local Anglia TV news!

In the years after the strike the campsite was closed so a group of us would pitch up amongst the dunes and become freelance pickers, which gave us a bit of power. The dunes had plots where people had bought the land to build chalets but the MOD stopped this due to the erosion. We had a good relationship with the locals until a group of new age travellers heard we were there and came en masse with their lorries and buses. We carried on going but it became more and more unfriendly so we eventually stopped. The new agers stayed and for years were moved from plot to plot by court injunctions until eventually they moved onto a plot whose owner was sympathetic to their plight. They are still there to this day; it's called "The Pit" and the original vehicles are still lived in although they don't go on the road anymore.

CHAPTER 5

SPUD BASHING IN ST DAVIDS PEMBROKESHIRE

Rhys with spanner Tony with smile

There were a number of jobs that I didn't like and most of them required being bent double or crawling on your hands and knees. Potato picking was well up there on the list of least favourite. Having said that, it was my favourite place to be so I grinned and bore it. On the coast, with some fantastic scenery and beaches, there was never a better setting to go to work. An early start meant an early finish so there was always time to go to the beach or into the town for a coffee or beer.

In the early days we worked at Creoswdig, but there were always other farms desperate to get pickers and during breaks in picking on one farm you could go to another. Creoswdig was a safe haven and all the travellers were well known to one another, which made for a very relaxed and fun atmosphere. It was a very sad day when Creoswdig was sold and, although it was in November, a few of us travelled down to help with the move.

With Creoswdig gone, we were forced to find another farm and didn't waste much time landing a job at one just up the coast. Many of the friends didn't join us on the new farm, choosing other areas of Britain or abroad to find work. With new 'colleagues' to meet, it was always a nervous time and this was compounded when the farmer informed us not to even look at "Rocky", whose reputation was well known to us as a violent Irish traveller! His time was up when a group of locals came over one night and asked him to leave the area. I will let you imagine how friendly that meeting was!

Potato pickers, as with any harvesting work, comes in many guises. Some are born into it and for others it's a lifestyle choice. For me the latter applied. On the first day of our new job we would see all types of travellers and some with harsh lives. One rather large chap with his petite wife and three kids under ten and one fifteen plus was, we learned, not a traveller but a someone who came out of his council house in summer to take advantage of the abundant work at harvest time. He was not alone in his attitude to his family; they were there to work and he wasn't! The morning started with him getting first dibs on the rows. This entailed him looking at the crop as it was riddled to choose the rows with most potatoes. He would then point to the row and his wife and kids would in turn fall to their knees and start filling their baskets. He would then collect the sacks, place them in the rows and then sit down only moving to collect more empty sacks so as to keep the family working. The man would collect the wage every night and retire to the pub. After a few days we realised that the eldest boy slept and ate under the caravan. We were told he was the lady's son from a previous marriage.

Picking was usually from 8 till 1 and I struggled with every minute. I soon jumped at the opportunity to start weighing and tying the sacks in readiness for the lorry. I would pick in the early part of the morning, 25p per 25kg bag, with my partner until there were enough bags to weigh and then switch to day rate (£3.80 per hour) till done. My girlfriend was good at picking so her day would finish at 1, whereas mine could go on till 3.

Visits from pickers on other farms were a daily event but not all of these were welcome. Irish travellers were a particular annoyance as they either wanted to find a wife, buy your vehicle or hassle you into a bare knuckled fight for money! Of course, you had to put up with all the rude comments when you refused a fight.

Although there were one or two tough guys, the majority of pickers were decent and we formed many friendships that last to this day.

CHAPTER 6

ITINERANT CHARACTERS

Baldy Pat

Life as an itinerant attracted many unsavoury characters. Some were on the run from the law, some were anti-social and others had mental health problems. Although these people formed a small part of life on the road they do make for the best story telling; many I would never forget!

Angel Dave an Unsavoury Saviour

Dave was no angel, nor was his name Dave! Angel Dave was of the motorcycle types of Angel and his name was Gordon – Angel Gordon, which doesn't have the same ring. For reasons of anonymity (and a touch of fear), I am not going to let you know where Angel Dave hails from. Nor where I saw him many years later chasing a woman down the high street threatening to kill her. I make no excuse for ducking into a Christian bookshop, a sanctuary, to hide. He was an exceptionally strong lean chap and more than once I was on the wrong end of his fury. He once held me off my feet with his fist pulled back ready to strike! He had the usual tattoos but the one on his back was the most memorable; it was done very badly with sloping sentences and the letters of differing sizes. The tattoo read - "Though I walk through the valley of death I fear no evil 'cause I am the evilest Mother….er you will ever meet."

Angel Dave was not the cleverest of souls, preferring to batter you into his way of thinking rather than discuss them. He took a major dislike to one of our group who, due to his constant use of cannabis, every roll-up would be loaded. We nicknamed him Sleepy John. Sleepy John had long greasy hair which, with head always looking at the ground, hung in front of his face. Sleepy John was the most inoffensive man you would ever meet but due to his lack of interaction made him a target for the likes of Angel Dave. Sleepy John grunted answers to questions and his mumblings were hard to follow, which made Angel Dave see red and on a few occasions he would explode, which usually meant a hand round the throat or sitting astride the victim with his fist about to fall. We intervened on numerous occasions but diplomacy rather than physical restraint was the way to go with this violent ignoramus. I hear you thinking why did they put up with any of this? Well we lived in a caravan in a field, or an orchard, and had no say who could come and work.

It was late at night. Six of us in total were around a campfire and Sleepy John was, quite deliberately, on the opposite side of the fire to Angel Dave. Conversation was flowing, Sleepy John was in his usual stupor, everything was normal. Sleepy John was standing, whilst Angel Dave was crouched. Suddenly without any warning, Angel Dave sprang like a gazelle across the fire and on top of Sleepy John. We all immediately grabbed Angel Dave who was shouting something. It took a while for us to realise Sleepy John's wellington boots had caught fire and Angel Dave was putting it out. Angel Dave had humanity despite himself.

There were some serious repercussions with that event. We were tolerated and even liked by some of the locals and they were our first point of call for help with Sleepy John. The on-call doctor refused to come to the site to help so we took him to A&E. The doctor was reported by the locals and was struck off as a result. Sleepy John had nasty burns to his leg where the rubber had melted. He went home to his parents to recoup and rejoined us at the next farm. Although Angel Dave was a hero for a while we were pleased he left shortly after to terrorise someone else!

CHAPTER 7

NE'ER DO WELLS

It is fair to say that the travelling community attracted more than its fair share of 'Ne'er do Wells" and unfortunately this was always what the local community heard about. I remember meeting a local girl who said parents warned their daughters that the travellers were coming. I eventually married that girl!

There are so many characters and incidents that this short piece can do justice to. For every bad egg there were a dozen decent people trying to make a living whilst being discriminated against at every turn. Some travellers revelled in this notoriety and would swagger around the local town rubbing the locals up the wrong way. "New age travellers " were probably the worst in their anti-establishment ways but were, in the main, decent types with some weird and wonderful vehicles and dress sense. My hat was firmly in that ring as a long-haired hippy.

When arriving in a place, there would be lot of police helicopter activity, which was a way for the police to monitor our whereabouts, count how many travellers were at the different farms and to check number plates for any vehicles involved in crime. We tried to make it difficult by hiding our number plates. We also made gestures towards the heavens. It is said that crime goes up immeasurably when travellers move into an area but this never told the true picture as local criminals would become more active during the "picking season" so as to blame the newcomers. A classic case was when a load of outboard engines were stolen from boats on the water. The police soon realised that the travellers they had photographed didn't have boats. They quickly traced the culprit selling them on at car boot sales in The Midlands. A good example of police monitoring helping the travellers.

People had great names often pre-fixed or followed by something they are known for which could be a specific look or a trait. This would separate people with the same name and many would have little idea of their "tag" - *Baldy Pat* (no prize for that one), *Ginger Rob* (again no prize), *Toothless Tony*, also known as *Central Eating*. Traits included *Monotone Pete*, *Sleepy John*, and *Angel Dave*. Other names included *Harry The Hat*, *Foreman Mart* (once coined for me) and *Truckles Tim*. Anyway you get the picture.

There are many stories, some funny, some awful and some tragic, but the most interesting were often the awful ones and as an example here's one that covers all three:

Itinerant work was often, and still is, a hide-out for criminals running from the police. This particular story involves a nasty man who was told by his friends "Go potato picking they will never look for you there." The family, Dad (Andy), Mum (Pam) and two young girls arrived at the farm in St Davids, in an old Ford mobile shop-type van curtained windows all round and looking forever like hippy travellers. As always, new people were welcomed in and tea offered, like a new neighbour would be. A few days went by and the new people blended in nicely with the usual rounds of visiting fires and stories being exchanged. There was no way of knowing what was to unfold over the coming weeks....... Late one evening Pam came and sat round the campfire and asked if I could go with her hubby to fetch a caravan they'd bought from somewhere near Fishguard. Their van had a tow hitch but no lights and they wondered if I would drive behind them. Fortunately for me, I had rather a large van and once we had arrived we mainly used bikes to get to town. Having got a refusal, Pam went around the site until Toothless Tony agreed to accompany them. I have to say in hindsight it was a bit strange - why not go in the day?

The next night they set off to get the caravan and after a couple of hours, Tony appeared at our campfire and explained what had happened.

"The police stopped Andy and Pam to warn them they had no lights," he said. Tony, not being a fan of the police, had driven off and left them to it. Another hour went by until Andy and Pam turned up towing the caravan. After a rant at Tony for leaving them it transpired the police had driven behind them all the way to the farm!

Now that was funny enough but what happened next was beyond belief. The caravan, as we started to suspect, had been stolen from a driveway just outside Fishguard. It belonged to none other than the helicopter police observer. They came to arrest them after picking mid-afternoon. The amount of police used was, we thought, over the top but it was not just about the caravan. The two children, who were living with their father, had disappeared with their mother and new partner we knew as Andy. "Andy" had been on Crime Watch and was wanted for credit card fraud and, of course, child abduction!

CHAPTER 8

OMEGA 3 SUPPLEMENTS

Martin and Pat off fishing!

Supplementing your income was a necessity and indeed a badge of honour. There were many ways to do this - some legal and some illegal. This one involves fishing, hence the title, and it had on-going, unforeseen consequences!

We had a small Mirror class dinghy with a temperamental outboard engine, which over the years gave us many tales to tell. The boat was owned by Baldy Pat who assured us he'd done navigation courses. Of course, for small fishing trips out of the harbour and as long as you didn't roam too far, this knowledge was not really needed. Baldy Pat was an adventurer and he couldn't resist trips further afield which could have ended in disaster. We would go out in the boat most evenings after all the chores were done post-picking and it was great fun. There was the obligatory leak or five but they were slow and we always had a baling bucket if it got bad!

Launching from Porth Clais near St Davids was always a challenge, as we were meant to pay mooring fees. It also involved getting wet and, with an audience of holiday makers, always involved a lot of uncontrollable, embarrassed laughter. To start with, we would wear our picking clothes as it was a good opportunity to get the excess mud off our trousers. We would arrive in a transit van with the boat on the roof. Due to our eagerness, we would never rely on the tide, so dragging the boat through sludge a half mile to the water was a common occurrence. We were mainly fishing for mackerel and, being the season, we were extremely successful. We also had a line out for the elusive but very profitable sea bass but in all the years we fished there the only other type of fish we caught was a scad - its other name of course is horse mackerel!

Mackerel are not the cleverest of fish, so hooks with silver paper were the preferred bait and with four per line, when you found a shoal there were rich pickings. The boat was slowly filling up with water so it was ideal to keep the catch alive which was very important not only for freshness but we could put the unsold fish back. The idea would be to catch as many as possible in a couple of hours, take them back and sell them to tourists on the quay side for 25p each (the going rate then). We would earn enough for a "sundowner" at the Farmers Arms, where we could catch up on any news with friends from other farms.

On one day off we decided to fish further afield and motored down to the next harbour, Solva, which turned into more of an adventure than anticipated. We tied the boat at the nearest point as possible to the village, then walked through the sludge to the slipway and on to a café/gallery. We bumped into some friends and went for a pint. Baldy Pat as it happened misread the tide table; the tide was coming in not going out! When we eventually went back to the to the harbour we couldn't see the boat as it had sunk! My boots that I had left on board were bobbing out to sea. It took a further three hours to be able to retrieve the boat and set off home.

On the way out to open water, we were passing small fishing boats coming in, as we found out, to shelter from the storm. We had gone past the point where it would be safe to turn the boat around and had to head for a large rock to turn. I could not believe how rough the sea had become. It was at this point, with a howling albeit nervous laugh, Pat announced he couldn't swim and that he would 'have to sink to the bottom and walk' or 'drink the f…ing lot'. We managed to turn round and head back into the harbour and hitch home, smelling of fish and drenched through to the bone.

CHAPTER 9

SELLING FRIDGES TO ESKIMOS

Overheads on the road after day-to-day living was really confined to the vehicle and trailer. Picking, unless you were very good, was not a big earner and could have become even less so in the mid eighties, when the government of the time tried to tax pickers.

It was a complicated system, and as realised, open to abuse. If my memory is correct the farm was allowed to claim a certain amount against tax for casual workers and it was left to the farmer to 'self assess'. The idea was as a casual worker you would have to ask for work every day and the farmer would record your name and the amount paid out. Farms claiming for harvest work but having nothing to harvest started cropping up and after some court cases it was decided to put the onus on the worker, as say a self-employed person. Names were taken! This of course was open to abuse and judging by one wage slip I saw, Luke Skywalker was alive and well picking potatoes in Pembrokeshire! Of course that worked fine if your first name was Luke and many people got caught out by the farmer. My favourite was Martin Chivers so there was a footballer somewhere being chased for tax on earnings from potato picking!

Paying tax on the pittance one could earn scrabbling in the mud picking potatoes was an insult to us and to add to this, some farms would deduct tax at source which did not go down well. Knowing the farmer had to get the crop in, there were a few walkouts over this; after all, who knew the money was going to the taxman.

As a sub-standard picker in everything but Victoria plums, I was happy to have a partner who not only picked well but seemed to enjoy doing so, pitting her self against hardened pickers to keep up. I soon became aware of another way of earning money which didn't mean suffering the aches and pains of being bent double or carrying 30lb of fruit around for the majority of the day. I started to sell potatoes at car-boots and markets around Pembrokeshire and even though everyone said "it's like selling fridges to Eskimos", I did very well. I did a Saturday and Sunday car-boot north of the county selling, at the height, a ton of potatoes (40 x 25kg bags) at £1.25 per 10lb bag on each day. Paying the farmer £2.50 cash left a good margin for me. Of course the earlier in the season, the more I would pay but the more I could charge. I would do a mid-week market in the south of the county near Tenby. As an extra earner I would buy plants from the car-boots up north and sell them on the Tenby market. This in turn was good, as I had the most landscaped caravan at the farm!

I did however ruffle a few feathers. I decided to try a market closer to the farm at Haverfordwest and in what became known as the "potato wars", I inadvertently clashed with a large local greengrocer who had a franchise on the same market. To be honest, it scared me big time! They were so threatening I could not open up as I was on my own and feared for my life and that of my van. They threatened to smash the vehicle up and said they could not guarantee my safety. I thanked them for their advice and left. Being younger and more full of it I didn't leave it there. I wrote a strong complaint to the owners of the site, Pembrokeshire Horticultural Society who, bless them, gave me a slot at the market and told the greengrocer they were not to sell potatoes that day! From then on, any new market I tried, if they were there, they would point to the exit with a smile. It was funny that they were on the Tenby market but, with no franchise, would come over and chat like old mates, "now't stranger than folk".

I also started a door-to-door potato selling round which went surprisingly well and would have carried on but for a personal disaster, which meant I had to leave Pembrokeshire for a while.

CHAPTER 10

PLUM PICKING IN THE VALE

Campfire cooking

But for the distance from the sea, plums were my favourite fruit to pick. The smell, taste and look of plum orchards delight me to this day. I worked on many farms in and around Evesham but unlike apple picking, which dragged on for an eternity from mid-August to mid-to-late November, plums were over much too quickly.

Starting with under ripe Yellow Egg, or their proper name Yellow Pershore, and ending with Marjorie's Seedling and Burbank, the orchards could be quite oppressive in the heat but the potential to earn mega bucks with Victorias, was enormous. To get to the Victorias in late August, there were many Yellow and Purple Pershores to pick. Purple and Yellow Eggs were always picked under-ripe to be used for jam. These would be picked in 40lb. wooden bushel boxes stacked onto a tractor and trailer, then trundled to Frank Idiens in Evesham. As these were picked under-ripe, unless you hunted down an earlier plum like Prolifics, you would need to wait to eat your first plum and I remember the frustration well.

My first experience of plum picking was at Machine Farm in Fladbury, near Evesham in 1973 at the tender age of seventeen. I went with a good friend and we arrived from Norfolk on push-bikes, this being a few years before I had learnt to drive. There was a pecking order and with long hair, patched jeans and a tent, we soon realised we were at the bottom. The farmer drove us to where people were picking, then he asked us to just watch for a few minutes. The image in front of us was hippies sitting under trees, playing guitars and smoking rather long cigarettes. One chap fell off the ladder, followed by the picking basket which had been balanced precariously on the top rung. He seemed all right until the basket and all the fruit landed on his chest, winding him. I must admit to feeling a little uneasy to be associated with them. Mr. Bird said if we thought we could do better than this 'shower' then grab a basket and get picking! We took up the challenge.

The next morning we arrived in the yard at the designated time. There were Gipsies, Asians, locals and hippies standing around in groups and the pecking order was about to be realised. A loud phone in the yard started to ring and was answered somewhere in the farm house. Several minutes later the farmer appeared and walked over to the Gypsy group which, after a few words, jumped into their vans and left. Next, the locals got the nod, then the Asians and finally, what seemed like an eternity, the hippies and we were given the order to pick.

After a few days I was asked if I could drive a tractor; "yes I said" (lying), "but never one of these - show me the controls."

Luckily the Massey Ferguson was simple to operate and after a few days I became competent, at two miles an hour! My mate loaded the boxes on to the trailer and after a few more days' practice, it was off to Evesham with a full load.

Throughout the 70s and early 80s we tried various farms around Evesham but were always bottom of the pile. Another problem was other groups would get to the orchard very early and steal the fruit on the bottom of all our trees!

Finding a fruit farmer with no pickers was heaven. After bouncing from one farm to another, we saw an advert in Norton post office window: 'Pickers wanted urgently'. Mrs. Williams and her odd son Arthur were mainly tomato growers but had an orchard of Victoria plums and no idea what to do with it. We kept our main job at Twyfords, now a shopping centre, and in the evenings went to Mrs. Williams, picking as much fruit as possible before taking it to Birmingham market in the early hours. These were exhausting times but the following year we were able to reap the rewards and became Mrs.

Williams' regular pickers. This lasted for five glorious years until one season poor old Mrs. Williams was intimidated enough to allow another group of travellers on her land. This was the death knoll for us, because Mrs. Williams chopped the trees down, I think out of fear.

I was then invited to pick for Dunsbys at Cotswold Orchard and that is where I stayed for many fruitful years, picking plums, pears, apples and eventually pruning the trees.

Maurice Perrys at Norton Evesham: we were very aware as the 'new kids on the block' that our role was to pick what the regulars didn't want. This usually meant the old orchards with less fruit so as you could imagine much grumbling ensued.

CHAPTER 11

CHERRY-MINDING

Half an hour before dawn on an early July morning, I wake up, look at the clock and slide out of bed. I have spent the whole night slipping in and out of sleep waiting for this moment and, to be honest, I'm relieved it is here. My eyes are starting to adjust to the lack of light as I move into the kitchen area and fumble for a candle. Once lit, I locate the kettle and curse the fact that it is empty, which means stepping outside where the water butt perches on a pile of logs. There's a slight chill in the air, no cloud cover so no rain; things are looking up. The water pours slowly and I start to get goose bumps. Once full, I start to turn the tap off, dislodging the butt from its precarious position. It falls tap first to the ground which shoves half an inch of mud up the spout. After turning the butt upright, I step back into the kitchen, slipping out of my boots and leaving them on the step.

At this point I should tell you that home is a 1950s 22ft. Cresta caravan rescued from a council tip, where it was used as a site office. The inside has been altered for permanent living. There's a double bed at the back of the van, running width-ways and raised to provide storage. Next is the living room, a long bench seat under the window on one side and opposite is the wood burner with a small seat to the side. A set of drawers is situated under a window on the other side of the burner. At the end of the bench seat is a small coffee table and at right-angles, approximately two-thirds of the caravan width, is a wall of built-in shelving; this would have been the pull-down bed when it was built. Moving through the gap between the shelves and the opposite wall, you enter the kitchen, with small gas and battery-run fridge, gas stove with oven, plenty of storage space and a sink so small it's a relief there's no running water to use it. Dish washing is done outside.

Back in the caravan, kettle on, I start to look for appropriate clothing for hanging around all day. Then a visit to the loo, which is a large hole in the ground with a rather low tarpaulin slung over a wooden frame, each family having their own. It is not too far to go to work - forty steps due-east of the caravan, but leave your post at your peril. The work place consists of a car seat, set on pallets to give it height, and in front, a long stick with a series of wires running every which way around the orchard. As an onlooker you may wonder at this set up until, that is, the long stick is pulled back as far as possible then released, where upon a staggered crescendo of clangs and bangs will ring out from every part of the Cherry Orchard. This is then followed by another staggered and much quieter echo from the hills beyond. Welcome to the crazy world of cherry-minding circa 1995!

The start of the procedure was to secure the purchase of the fruit for the season and this happened at blossom time. The owners had long since given up on harvesting their own crop and all the hassle that involves, so they devised an ingenious way of getting someone else to do it whilst still making a bit of cash. Here's how it worked (and may still do):

A number of interested parties would gather in the orchard at blossom time and they would 'bid on the blossom', the highest getting the fruit for the season. For most of the bidders, it would be a case of deciding what the crop was going to be like but our bid would start from the point of having a place to live for a number of months. As itinerants, we travelled from one farm job to the next and having a safe place to stay was paramount, especially as we were often confused with new age travellers with our long hair and green painted lorries and caravans; not as silly as you may think as they blended into the countryside. The fruit of course was important but we had a double reason for winning the bid. Orchard secured, it was back to St Davids in Pembrokeshire to the potato harvest and a wait until it was time to move in to the orchard.

Dawn at any time of year is a very magical time but dawn in summer and in an orchard has a certain resonance with animals and humans alike. It's the anticipation of the crop ripening and the feast ahead. We humans, of course, pick the fruit from the tree, package it, transport it and then sell it on to other humans. Birds and other flying things, such as wasps, feed straight from the tree and here lies the problem; how do we keep the birds off the crop? Of course you can put nets on the smaller trees and the use of polytunnels is widespread these days, but what about the huge trees? This is where cherry-minding comes into play! Position taken, tea in hand and a good book, your shift begins. Happy in the knowledge that it is a shift and you will be relieved mid-morning, you enjoy your surroundings while you can as it won't be long before you are sick to death of the place.

You take your first draw on the roll-up, which will be your friend until people start to wake up, and after the late night who; knows when that will be. You pick up the stick and think about pulling it. You hesitate, but there's no justification to start the racket as people are still asleep. The unwritten protocol of cherry-minding is do not make a noise unless it is essential, which it will be soon. It is 5 am and the telegraph wire is starting to fill up with starlings, the scourge of the cherry-minder. Not only are the cherries very tasty, but they act like a drug to the birds who go into a frenzy when they ripen and you could lose your crop in no time. This will go on for weeks but more direct methods will be used later.

A few days and Slug arrives. Now, I'm not sure why he's called Slug, but maybe it is because he drinks a lot or as I have never seen him wash his slimy self! For a slab (twelve cans) of special brew, food and an hourly rate, Slug will take over the minding for a number of hours respite. So with Slug in place and the birds getting bolder, it's time for the motorcycle minus the silencer. This is great fun for a while but, as each thing is introduced, the birds get used to it. We employ a pest controller; well, a gun-toting hooligan as it turns out. Anthony is a local farmer's son who has a licence for proper guns to cull deer. He also has an array of other weapons and it makes one uneasy sitting with him. He starts shooting birds flying over the orchard for fun. This is not fun if you are cooking on an outside fire and not quite dead birds are falling from the sky. Another group of cherry-minders down the road had an accident with a shotgun. Whilst dashing around in a pick-up, the guy in the passenger seat has the shotgun resting barrel down on his foot. While bouncing around the orchard the gun goes off... Anthony is very proud of his work and sleeps by the fire so he can be at it at first light. We offered blankets which he declined and proceeded to pull some manky blankets from the back of his pickup. Underneath was that day's kill!

I soon realised that the 'park-up' (where you stop and set up camp) was more important than the cherries so we started buying in from other orchards. We would pick from our orchard but all but stopped dealing with the starlings. We were a bit naughty in that we never mentioned that not all the cherries came from our orchard. Selling in lay-bys in those days was the norm and finding a good vacant one was like gold dust. We looked long and hard and eventually found a lay-by on the A23 to Hastings and, as luck would have it, there was another one opposite. Setting up my daughter, aged sixteen and her cousin, seventeen, in both lay-bys was a dream, with lots of traffic heading for the coast, especially on weekends. The other bonus was they came back on the same road, so the evening was even better as people bought for friends and family. During the week, coaches full of elderly people on day trips to the coast would be our big earner, so an early start and late finish was essential. Every night I would drive to Faversham to fetch cherries, which would always be bought for cash, for the morning and again midday for the evening 'rush'. It was even better when it rained, as the cherries tended to split quite readily and the price reflected this. In those days people were much more laid back when it came to the look of the fruit and if you could offer cheaper cherries all the better!

Unfortunately, there was a lot of unrest at the camp as the other workers who had heard what could be earned wanted a turn at selling in the lay-by. This was disastrous as customers would flock to young, tidy and enthusiastic sellers but not to scruffy, rude pickers. After much arguing, I decided to pull my family out. We returned to Pembrokeshire and never went back to Kent.

CHAPTER 12

AN INTINERANT'S LOT

Time to move again

I have compiled below a list of jobs through the year.

Due to the nature of the work, I would count my year from the start of pruning as this is when my winter work began.

November/December

Pack-house, pruning and cider-making, Vale of Evesham. Once I had decided that this was what I wanted to do I settled in to it for many years.

Previously I had worked in forestry, camping in woods, felling silver birch trees for pulp. This would last from November to March. The work was hard and the living conditions harder but the main reason for stopping was the amount of chainsaw accidents I saw. Of course, in those days safety features on chainsaws were limited.

December

With my forestry connections, I spent a number of years felling and selling Christmas trees; something I returned to when I settled in to home ownership.

January

The new year saw pruning in earnest with rainy days in the pack-house and a day a week pressing cider. Daffodils in Cornwall was a one-off as they gave me a rash.

February

Pruning and pack-house duties carried on but we always took a week out to go to Pembrokeshire to plant potatoes. Although this was a cold time of year, the break from pruning was great and we treated it as a holiday. The caravan would be left in the orchard and we would take the spare room (also known as a transit van) to the seaside!

March

All pruning now. We did some spring onion-picking for a season. I couldn't understand how anyone could make a living at 1p per bunch! Bidding on the cherry blossom would straddle the months of March and April.

April

Pruning of the plum trees would begin now. This was also time for hop-tying in Leigh Sinton, Worcestershire and we did this for a few years prior to pruning work. Hops grow anti-clockwise and the idea was to tie the young shoots around five wires. After a few weeks you would return to retie the ones that had fallen off.

May

Time to move to St Davids for the start of potato-picking and selling.

June

Well into the potato season now. Driving tractors for the hay harvest proved a welcome break. Mid to the end of June saw a massive journey to Norfolk for the strawberry season. For a few years we travelled to Kent to do the cherry minding, picking and selling.

July

From mid-July it was time to summer prune. This entailed pulling out water shoots to allow the sun to ripen the fruit.

August

The long awaited plum season started, which was where I earned my biggest wage packets.

Early September
Plums and a few early apples.

Mid September
The start of the apple season in earnest. To get the crop into storage, we worked from 8am or 9am on Sundays till 4.30pm, seven days a week through October and in to November. Any breaks would see us in St Davids.

October
Apples are go! All of this month is taken up with the apple harvest. Getting the Cox crop into storage meant long hard days.

Throughout my life as an itinerant, I did many other jobs including, in the early days:

tree-felling in Kesteven Forest, Lincolnshire

Christmas trees in Leicestershire

raspberries in Scotland - too many midges!

picking sprouts and other vegetables in Worcestershire

hop-picking in Worcestershire

digging drains in Sea Palling, Norfolk

CHAPTER 13

1994

Lay-by nightmares

The following chapter is concerning the Criminal Justice Bill (CJB) which had a major effect on the ability of itinerants and other travellers to move freely around the country. Whilst I hold a view on the rights or wrongs of the CJB, I only write here of its effect on myself and fellow itinerants. There are books on the events leading up to the CJB of which I list some below for the reader to make their own decision.

It had always been the case that lay-bys and common ground were places that travellers would park for periods of time but in my case this was limited to lay-bys and usually overnight. Lay-bys were also a place to park whilst waiting for the farmer to allow you onto his land. Many locals did not like travellers parked at the side of the road as rubbish could accumulate and, in some cases, left when the travellers moved on. In all my time as an itinerant parking in lay-bys, I was never offered a rubbish collection service and always disposed of my rubbish before moving on. The 1994 CJB allowed only twelve hours parking in lay-bys and limited the amount of vehicles allowed at any one time. This impacted massively on my ability to move around the country and would mean moving from one farm to another, often in one go.

Shortly after the Bill was passed, I moved from Evesham to St Davids when, at Sennybridge in Wales, I hit a pot-hole which severed one wheel from my twin-axled caravan. I pulled into a lay-by and my friend travelling behind followed. In what seemed like seconds, we were confronted by angry locals who, having read the new Bill wrongly, called the police. I wish I had taken that officer's name to thank him for his help to defuse the situation and point out that the illegal act would be for us to pull out of the lay-by with an unroadworthy trailer! With the locals dispersed, the officer set about helping us sort the problem out. In twenty years of travelling I have never been so frightened as at that time.

We had many confrontations whilst moving around the countryside after the CJB was passed in to law. One notable event was at Moreton-in-the-Marsh in Gloucestershire. We returning from seeing my daughter in Norfolk, heading for Evesham, when we turned into the high street at Moreton-in-the-Marsh and found ourselves at the end of a group of "new-age travellers" involved in a pitched battle with police. I had no idea how it started, who was right or wrong, but as I saw a number of police heading for us in our brightly coloured van, my girlfriend with braided hair and me with long hair, I feared the worst. With the last two vehicles before us having had their windscreens smashed, I jumped out to talk to the officers, having convinced them we were not a threat. We were turned around to find a different route to Evesham. I could have stood my ground but without knowing the reasons for the trouble it was not my place to argue.

As a result of the CJB, many people I know moved to the continent where they believed itinerant working was easier and many are still there. Indigenous itinerants are a rare sight indeed with many now coming from Eastern Europe. This suits many employers as they come via agencies, modern day gangers, with no strain on resources as they live off the farm in shared houses and caravans. Many people say that British workers don't want the work but this is unfair. With the cost of mortgages, council tax and vehicle costs, it is impossible to survive on the money offered and travellers with little overheads will always be the backbone of harvest work. The arrival of Eastern Europeans has always been contentious but without them there is no one left to pick your fruit and vegetables!

CHAPTER 14

HEALTH & SAFETY

Health and safety

The two words which, when put together sent a chill down the spines of some farmers and pickers, were *Health* and *Safety*. Those two words always came with a cost; for the farmer it meant upgrading equipment and for the picker it could mean earning less money as farmers would try to claw back these costs. Of all the pickers' equipment, the ladders were the most important as regards to health and safety. I saw, and was involved in, many accidents with ladders but only one with a 'bodger' (picking bucket) and that was as a consequence of falling off a ladder.

We were picking damsons at what was then Hilliers Fruit Farm, now Twyfords Garden Centre. We were down by the River Avon, a gang of about five with my daughter Libby aged eight and her cousin Josh nine, where there were a number of incidents on the same day. The first was Baldy Pat falling from his ladder after a rung broke. It is quite awkward wearing your bodger, which was mainly for apples and pears, whilst picking plums so it was normal to perch it on the rungs of your ladder. Landing at the foot of the ladder and slightly shocked, the main danger was yet to come. The bodger dislodged, full of damsons and hurtled towards the ground, slamming in to Pat's chest, winding him. It took some time for him to recover and join in our uncontrollable laughter.

Later on that day, Josh came over for lunch and he was soaking wet. We were all in shock when he explained he'd fallen into the river and Libby had fished him out with a long stick! We never took them there again.

Tractors were also a hazard and some of the drivers' actions were incredulous. I was picking potatoes in Pembrokeshire for Emirys John (deceased), a hopeless drunk in charge of a potato riddler. My head was down, engrossed in the pain of picking, when Emirys appeared next to me on his knees explaining where I was to go next. I realised the tractor was still travelling with its riddler engaged, although this was normal practice. I was at the end of my row so the tractor had got to the end of its row. There was a massive noise and sparks were flying as the tractor mounted a large rock, careered down the other side and into a pond before spluttering to a halt. Another farmer doing the same thing went to jump back into the cab, slipped and got his foot stuck in the step. Being dragged down the row, he struggled to stop the tractor from ploughing into a car with kids in. Heroically, he threw his body under the wheel and the tractor stalled. He was hospitalised and off work for ages. It didn't stop the practice.

I have driven many un-roadworthy and frankly dangerous tractors in my time. Picking into one third of a ton boxes, they would be stacked in twos, ready for the tractors with front and rear mounted forks to ferry the boxes home. On the flat there was no problem, but going down hill with no brakes made it a hairy ride. To slow down, one would lower the front forks to slide along the track, which was a skill in itself if you didn't want to grind to a halt. Trailers loaded with apples were as bad if coming down a hill. I couldn't help but laugh as one of the trailer wheels passed me like in some cartoon! Luckily it was a twin axle, so no harm done.

A friend, 'Burning' Chris, was given the job of feeding the prunings on to a fire. This was done with a tractor mounted buck-rake. The trick was, with fresh wood, to keep the fire compact. To achieve this, wood would be placed on top of the fire and then the tractor would be driven up and down the pile compressing it. Chris was a mile away from the nearest help and managed to get the 'new' tractor stuck on the side of the fire pre-mobile phone days; he had to run a mile to get help. We saw him at the top of the hill waving and screaming. We set off towards him so you could imagine the amount of time the tractor was perched on the fire before another tractor was despatched to help! Amazingly, not too much damage to the tyres - well not enough to worry about changing them.

With chainsaws being passed around under one certificate, you can imagine how incredible it was that no one was killed, although some farmers were seriously hurt.

The use of sprays was always a hazard; not only the spraying itself but their disposal was a lot to be desired. Whilst pruning on a farm in Evesham, we were warned by a horn that the sprayer was coming up the row next to us. The sprayer had a massive fan on the back to help reach the top of the trees so it was like a large cloud of mist. It was close so we dropped our pruning equipment and ran to a safe distance. The old farmer who was with us stayed put, turned to one side and put a hand over his pipe! Remember at this time the sprays were awful and organo-phosphates were regularly used. The driver, whilst spraying, was safe sitting in an enclosed space but on one occasion there was not a tractor with a cab available so the old farmer put the sprayer on an old cab-less Ford. No horn warning this time, so after inhaling something obnoxious we ran. The old boy was in a cloud of his own!

Disposing of banned or out-of-date sprays was like a chemistry lesson gone wrong. Throwing glass jars of unknown liquid on to fires made with old tyres was the norm. Amazing how some farmers would claim to be the guardians of the countryside. Nowadays, the sprays have been improved in leaps and bounds but even so, mistakes are made. One farmer, name withheld, sprayed weed killer onto a few acres of apple trees. Needless to say, there were no apples that year!

CHAPTER 15

CHANGE OF DIRECTION

It became clear to me in the summer of 1996 that my time on the road was coming to an end. I had watched an increase in Eastern European labour which was making the amount of work available to indigenous itinerants becoming less each year, so more people after fewer jobs.

We decided to stay in Pembrokeshire, focusing on selling produce at markets and, with the offer of a chalet to renovate and free rent in exchange for work, it seemed the writing was on the wall. I moved the caravan into the garden of the chalet and set about building a new home. For a number of months everything was fine; the chalet was coming along well, I had started a new door-to-door potato selling round, the markets were proving interesting and my girlfriend landed a job milking. Life was good without any whiff of the bombshell around the corner.

My girlfriend and I decided to get married and, with a reception at the chalet and honeymoon in Southern Ireland, it seemed the transition from traveller to house-dweller was complete. In November of that year a letter arrived, pushed through the door of the chalet, which would signal a return to life in a caravan. It turned out my wife of a few months was having an affair with the kind farmer who had given us the chalet. So much for a 'normal life'. I returned to the farm in Evesham to start a season of pruning but with coaxing from friends in Pembrokeshire I returned to St Davids. I rented a cottage and spent the working week in Evesham and weekends in Pembrokeshire. In May 1998, I met Trina who lived in Fishguard. After a while, we decided I would move into her house. I was still travelling between Worcestershire and Pembrokeshire and this was becoming increasingly difficult, so in 2000 we made the permanent move to Cheltenham in Gloucestershire, where we had a son and got married.

I still work on farms I had contact with whilst travelling, which takes me to Pembrokeshire, Worcestershire, Somerset, Oxford and Hereford so I guess the travelling instinct remains, although I always come home to a *House*!